Writing WRONGS

2018

Strength in Vulnerability:

Reclaimed Voices of

Domestic Violence & Sexual Assault

A publication by college and university students

Contact

P.O. Box 3
Virginville, PA 19564
dawn@seekreporttruth.com

Website

seekreporttruth.com

Social

@seekreporttruth

@seekreporttruth

@seek_report_truth

The mission of Writing Wrongs is to generate awareness and promote understanding of various social issues by providing an immersion experience for student multimedia journalists. They produce an entire print book about the specified topic in one weekend.

Copyright © 2018 Writing Wrongs
All image rights reserved.

All rights reserved. No parts of this book may be reproduced, in any form, without permission from the publisher, except for a reviewer who wishes to quote brief passages.

The views in this book are those of the authors and individuals and do not necessarily reflect the opinions or policies of the organizations or institutions included, mentioned, or advertised in the publication.

Published by
New Dawn Enterprises, LLC
newdawnenterprises.net

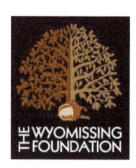

TABLE OF CONTENTS

Strength in Forgiveness	1
Damaged, but Not Broken	3
From Invisible to Visible	5
Finding Her Voice Again	9
It Haunts Me	11
"Scars Like White Tiger Stripes"	14
From Victim to Victor	16
Refusing to Lie	19
A Chorus No Longer Silenced	21
An Army of Identities: Coping with DID	25
Growing Beyond the Cracks	29
A Relentless Spirit	33
Healing Through Trauma	37
Survivor of Steel	38
"My Spirit"	41
Advocates Seeking Justice	42
Meet the Writing Wrongs 2018 Staff	44
Meet the Writing Wrongs 2018 Advisors	45
Humanitarian Social Innovations	46
Sponsors	47
"Fifteen"	52

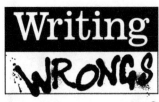

2018

Staff

Writers
Marissa Dunbar
Tyler James McMaster
Alexyss Panfile
Amanda Paradis
Maria Travato
Adam Varoqua
Michaela Yurchak

Print Designers
Jay Burton
Nina Renna

Photographer
Matthew Ludak

Social Media Manager
Carlee Nilphai

Advisors

Founder & Project Manager
Dawn Heinbach

Writing/Editing
Colleen Clemens
Michelle Kaschak
Anne Mahar
Janae Sholtz
Donna Singleton

Print Design
Gayle F. Hendricks

Photography
Jane Ammon

Social Media
Jessica Hughes

Strength in Forgiveness

By Amanda Paradis

Letting go of trauma is something many abuse survivors have trouble doing. Jessie Santiago was fortunate enough not only to escape her abuse but to find closure and happiness as well. She first experienced physical and sexual abuse at a young age. Initially, she thought this was just how children were treated. She thought, "I was being a real bad little girl and I was being punished." She came to realize this was not normal, but she was taught to "shut up about everything." Growing up, she had no support system – no one to confide in. Santiago finally built up the courage and trust to confide in a friend about the sexual abuse she endured. Her friend encouraged her to speak out about what was going on. Unfortunately, Santiago's mother did not believe her. Santiago stated, "The first words out of her mouth were 'You provoked him.'" According to Santiago, her mother's words "completely destroyed" her.

Shortly after confiding in her mother when she was 14, Santiago was kicked out of her house. Not having a place to live spurred her to move in and start a relationship with a 22-year-old man. Santiago became a wife "in a way," at a time she was not ready. Escaping her home was not escaping the abuse, however. She still endured physical abuse in her new home. This abuse became a pattern – a cycle she thought was going to continue for the rest of her life. The patterns of abuse led to a whirlwind of emotions. In her attempt to process her emotions, Santiago became depressed and searched for ways to fill the void. She turned to drugs and alcohol to numb the pain and became promiscuous in attempts to find love. She explained, "I didn't go about it the right way, but I didn't know any better."

Years passed before Santiago began her healing process. She spent many years depressed and tried to take her life several times. It was not until a friend introduced her to religion that she truly began to heal. She learned Jesus came to give salvation to all, and she no longer needed to suffer. In 2003, Santiago accepted the lord into her life and began her journey of healing. She was delivered from depression, acquired freedom, and forgave the people who hurt her. Forgiving those who hurt her, for her, does not mean condoning their abuse. Abusing someone physically,

emotionally, or sexually is never okay. However, some find strength in forgiveness. For her, healing started with Jesus. Santiago explained her healing had everything to do with her relationship with God. She stated, "It hasn't been easy in all these years, but you know what? Only God has given me the strength. ... I wouldn't have been here sharing my story with you if it wasn't for the lord."

Santiago's sexual abuse began when she was only 9 at the hands of her step father. She viewed him as her real father, the only male role model in her life. His abuse shattered her world and shattered her view of men. Since finding Jesus, Santiago has grown to forgive many people in her life, including her stepfather. At a family event, she approached him and shared that his abuse destroyed her. He started crying, sobbing, threw himself on his knees and asked for forgiveness. "I forgave him. I pray for this man because who knows what he went through. Everyone has a story." Forgiveness is a big part of what set her free and gave her closure. The most admirable characteristic about Santiago is her ability to forgive. She has every right to be angry with those who hurt her, yet she decides not to hold onto that anger. She understands everyone has struggles we cannot see, and their experiences may influence their actions.

Two prominent themes emerged from Santiago's story. The first is that everyone has a story to share. The second is that hurt people hurt people because they do not know how to express themselves. When it comes down to it, everyone is just searching for love.

Santiago was able to find love after all the hardships she endured. She has been happily married for 11 years. Santiago explained everything is different in her marriage. She never imagined she would be in a healthy relationship; though not perfect, it is different from her previous relationships. When asked if Santiago's younger self thought she would be as happy as she is now, she responded by saying her current situation was a dreamland or fantasy. She never thought she would be where she is today. Santiago stated, "I've been in the dark side and now I'm on this side – and oh my God, I never would've dreamt."

Denise Kuhns

Damaged, but Not Broken

By Adam Varoqua

The life of Denise Kuhns, 55, has been marked by tragedy and abuse as well as her continuous struggle for justice. To start with, the summer before Kuhns turned 11, she and her mother became members of a local church. Kuhns joined that church's choir and went on trips to different congregations.

Behind closed doors, though, this was no ordinary Sunday church. From the moment she joined until turning 18 years old, she became a witness to and victim of torture, rape, forced drugging, and other crimes of a violent cult.

"Torture. Rape. Abortions. Girls were impregnated. Abortions on the altar. The fetuses were thrown in the furnace in the basement," said Kuhns. She, along with many other victims, was also forced to have an abortion and was raped by the pastor at his home. Animal sacrifices and blood baptisms were commonplace as well. The pastor, who was the main perpetrator, was aided in this child abuse by other members of the church's hierarchy. What made this more difficult was how the church silenced the victims from ever speaking out.

"You didn't have a choice. You were programmed to commit suicide if you spoke of it, or they would kill you. And the way to commit suicide was to make it look like an accident," she said. Kuhns related how she didn't drive until she was 30 for fear of driving into a telephone pole, a fear instilled in her by her abusers. Kuhns also spoke of others who had committed suicide in her social circle.

The abuse didn't end at that cult though, and it didn't even begin there. Kuhns, along with her siblings, were sexually, physically, and emotionally abused by their mother. Since Kuhns was the oldest amongst her siblings, she helped to raise them through all of this.

Her cult abuse persisted through childhood into young adulthood. Though she was forced to leave the church after young adulthood because of the fear church officials had of her speaking out, her trauma continued into her three marriages. "Constantly through my life I've always been with abusive men," Kuhns said.

Her first husband was the result of an arranged marriage made by church officials and the husband's family. He was also one of the many victims of the cult's abuse. She related to how he was emotionally abused by his parents and how tightly he was controlled by them. They even exerted their control over Kuhns. As she explains, "If they said we had to be there, we had to be somewhere. They showed up to our honeymoon." She later discovered that they would stalk her after the marriage ended.

Her husband was mainly absent during the marriage, often at his parent's house, but at the times that they were together, he would be physically abusive, once even breaking her jaw. This marriage didn't last long. She married her second husband with whom she had all of her four children. Her second husband, however, was verbally and emotionally controlling over what she wore and loved to do. As she explained, "Not being allowed to wear certain things, or I used to sing a lot so being jealous of me singing and things like that."

She rekindled her relationship with her first husband after her second marriage was ending. He wasn't abusive to her or her children but committed animal abuse. Kuhns said, "He did cut off my cat's tail because he was being triggered by the cats, the sacrificing of the cats." As Kuhns related, her first husband didn't stay in the picture long this time as his emotional state started to deteriorate, and she didn't feel safe having him around her children.

"I could not deal with a 44-year-old who is acting like a 10-year-old, no matter how much I loved him," she said.

Her most recent (third) marriage also ended with divorce, as her third husband was controlling too and became physically abusive at the end of their relationship. In the midst of all these abusive experiences and

Denise Kuhns during her interview

raising her children, she was plagued by nightmares and flashbacks of the cult abuse she faced when she was a child. The flashbacks and nightmares stemming from the cult abuse started happening in the mid-90s, around the time other victims started coming forward with their stories. Unfortunately, their narratives fell on deaf ears, as Kuhns related: "The police never did anything about it."

It was after the first reports that Kuhns confided to a friend all the nightmares she was experiencing, which revealed that those nightmares were in fact based on her past traumatic experiences. Through that revelation, she became aware of her own victim status.

From then on, she has been in and out of therapy, suffering from PTSD and taking antidepressants and anti-anxiety medication. She expressed that whenever she speaks about her story, most do not want to hear it.

Kuhns eventually went back to the church and sought guidance with a new pastor who did believe her. This pastor wrote a letter to her doctor in 2002, relating what happened to Kuhns and others. In the letter, she says, "It is now a known fact that cultic rituals of a liturgical, sexual, and violent nature were secretly conducted here at [perpetrator location] by the then-pastor and others. Males and females of every age were victimized."

Since becoming aware of her victimhood, it has been nothing but struggle for Kuhns. Even with all this torment taking a toll on her, she has found the strength to keep seeking justice and telling her story, though the abiding feeling of strife and anguish is unmistakable. She also found the strength to confront the bishop and demand action. Recent events in the news have propelled her as she explained, "When all this exposure over at the Catholic Church came out, we figured — well, you know what I mean? It's time. Own up."

Still, nothing was done because the pastor is not working at that church anymore. Instead, he was promoted to the position of bishop, overseeing many other churches in the area.

It does not help that people around her have been dismissive as well. She explained, "They don't want to hear it. They don't question it — they just don't want to hear it." She admitted that a part of it is because the story of a cult in your hometown is not easy for people to accept, saying, "Nobody wants to believe this happened in their own city."

Her story is shocking and disheartening yet revealed the onus to report everything that she disclosed. She was raped repeatedly, abused mentally, physically, and sexually by those closest to her, and was routinely abused by cult members when she was a child and forced to have an abortion. Even with all this, her story was not listened to, until now.

She is the epitome of a survivor. "You write my story. You write my story, and if you want to write my book, you can write my book because this is coming out. People need to know that when somebody tells their story that they're not fucking crazy. Nobody can make this shit up, and we don't deserve to be shunned."

She mainly wants the readers to know this: "I want people to look at people like me and others in a different light. I realize that you know we are human beings, too. Just because we're damaged, we didn't live to our full potential, it doesn't make us less of a person, just different."

From Invisible to Visible

By Alexyss Panfile

At 51 years old, Yolanda Mendoza checked herself into Reading Rehab after being badly beaten by her boyfriend. By this time, she had suffered through the physical abuse of having her face slashed and ribs broken. On top of this, she had the weight of emotional baggage from being viciously berated.

"When I look back at my life, and I think of myself, it's almost like I was dead. I was in this dark pit, and I was dead," Mendoza, now 58, explained.

At that point, Mendoza had already suffered a lifetime of abuse. Although she had never witnessed domestic abuse growing up, her first memory of abuse came from being molested by her father at age 9. This started the belief that abusive behavior was okay, leading to a brutal cycle of relationships that would alter her life forever.

Mendoza's first abusive relationship was with the father of her three oldest children. She then married a man who also abused her verbally and physically.

Mendoza describes what this was like: "All of my life, I thought to be loved was to be beaten. To be loved meant that they loved you because they were jealous. Love was control. Love meant you were isolated."

In September of 2007, she was able to escape that marriage. This was after her husband tied her up with a belt for six hours and physically abused her to prevent her from attending her daughter's wedding. Although she escaped, she could not go to the wedding because she had to seek asylum at a domestic violence center. Unfortunately, this did not stop her husband from pursuing her. She moved from town to town and even state to state, and still he was able to find her.

Staff Writer Alexyss Panfile (left) interviews Yolanda Mendoza.

"Abuse was something that was very familiar to me," she explained with a sigh. "I just wanted to be loved. And because I wanted to be loved, it was a way of allowing men to love me."

Her second husband marked her third abusive relationship. Over the course of these relationships, she tried to take her life seven times. Mendoza recalled the chilling moment her husband at the time picked her up from the hospital and told her "parasites don't die."

partners spewed at her. She can only hope that the women she ministers will be able to find themselves as she did despite what they may have heard for years.

"Today I know I was created for a purpose," Mendoza said with a smile.

This new purpose would help countless men and women. She meets with other survivors in Reading, Pennsylvania at the Gathering Place, where they join in prayer and build relationships with each other. She

> ## "Society believes they know what you need, so they define you by what they believe you need — and so they make you invisible."

All of this led to Mendoza's addiction to crack cocaine and alcohol, as well as her continuous struggle with mental health. Her addiction escalated when she was told by authorities that "women like you get taken out in body bags."

Mendoza began to reach out to God because she was isolated from any support. On October 17, 2011, Mendoza pulled herself out of the denial she was in and realized her addiction was what was truly controlling her life in that moment. She left her abuser after she decided it was the last time he would terrorize her. Mendoza was then 51 and tired of it all when she decided to enter rehab.

While she was in Reading Rehab, she was encouraged to enter a different long-term rehab where she had her first real encounter with God. From there, her faith carried her along through her journey to freedom.

Today, Mendoza dedicates her time to her own ministry called Ashes to Beauty. She is a pastor who mentors women who have dealt with or are dealing with abuse and addiction. She shared that a lot of the women refer to her as "mom" because of the guidance she has provided them: "God has given me a burden to try to teach them you don't need to be this way because there's a better way of being loved."

When asked what she wants other survivors to know, she simply replied, "to have hope." Mendoza reminisced on the times she believed the horrible lies and insults her past

feels that building relationships with the men and women is an extremely important component to ministering them because she knows how hard it was to receive the right help when she was struggling.

Mendoza best relates that struggle as being invisible: "Society believes they know what you need, so they define you by what they believe you need — and so they make you invisible." She feels it is imperative to be there for the women and not to tell them what to do. Giving them options, she feels, allows them to choose what works best for them. In a piece she wrote about this feeling of being invisible, she says, "If you want to know my needs, get personal with me and know me beyond what you might see or assume. Please, know that I am visible."

Because she has been restored by the spirit of God, she no longer struggles with nightmares. Although her past will always be there in the back of her mind, she feels that she can live her life.

Mendoza concludes her thoughts by saying, "I'm not afraid to die because I was dead, and today I'm alive."

The day after this interview, she will marry her fiancé with whom she has had a healthy relationship for 5 years. She will be surrounded by her family and those in her ministry and will have the happy ending she deserved from the start.

#FactsMatter

On average, nearly 20 people per minute are physically abused by an intimate partner in the U.S.

Source: NCADV.org

Writing Wrongs 2018

Yolanda Mendoza

Theresa Margaret

Finding Her Voice Again

By Maria Trovato

Theresa Margaret's relationship with Joe did not begin as physically abusive. It started with manipulative and controlling behavior that transformed into verbal abuse, quickly transitioning into physical and sexual abuse. Before the relationship ended, he had tried to kill her multiple times.

Joe usually refrained from damaging Theresa's face, instead punching her in the head, kicking her in the abdomen, and smashing her head into picture frames. Holes riddled the wall from the impact of her body when he hit her. She suffered concussions which will affect her health for the rest of her life.

He would plunge her head into the sink when she was washing dishes, once when there were knives in the sink.

"It took years for me to be able to wash my knives again," she said.

Those around Theresa knew the relationship was unhealthy but were unaware of the full extent of the violence. During the relationship, she felt isolated and alone. In part, this was due to the fact that Joe's abuse extended to threats of her immediate family.

"I was very protective over my family because he very regularly told me what he wanted to do to my mom and my sister," she said. "The people who I could have confided in, I was really trying to protect from him."

When Theresa tried to leave, Joe would threaten to kill her, her children, and her other family members. However, Theresa realized she needed to escape the morning he was especially violent and ordered her to quit her job.

"He was losing control. That day, I had to make the choice," she said. "I knew that if I quit and went home, he was going to kill me and probably my kids."

Theresa left work early that day and removed her children from the house with the help of police. After a week of staying with her sister, she informed Joe that she planned to return to her house and that he needed to leave. She returned to find him there, with her things burned in a bonfire.

That night, Joe raped her at knifepoint twice and held her hostage with knives hidden in every room. The next morning, she managed to leave for work by convincing him that they would get back together. He then followed her and raped her at her place of work. Immediately afterwards, he attempted to force her to rob a bank with him, prompting her to report the situation to the police.

"This rape was so 'nothing' to me," she said. "Rapes with him were daily, so small and minuscule in the scheme of what he'd done that I almost forgot to bring it up."

Joe was ultimately sent to prison where he remains today. Theresa recognizes that she received justice through the legal system and that most survivors do

"They don't get to win."

not. However, when Theresa reported the incident to the police, she had no idea that the story of her rape at her place of work would end up on the front page of the local newspaper. Although the article published did not mention her by name, it mentioned where she lived and worked, making Theresa's identity clear to anyone who knew her.

"When the newspapers published my story without my permission, when they published my story that was in a way to get headlines, it really shut me up for quite a while because I was not ready," Theresa said. "Allowing my story to be in writing [with Writing Wrongs] is my next step to finding my voice in another way, in a way that was taken from me before."

Theresa's relationship with Joe was not her first experience with domestic abuse. She entered her relationship with Joe after leaving another abusive relationship with the father of her children. She has had five abusers throughout her life. It is common for domestic abuse victims to suffer from more than one abuser because

this type of violence leaves them susceptible to further abuse. Soon after Joe was sent to prison, she was date raped by another man.

Theresa struggled with many internal issues for a long time and was able to heal slowly through her relationship with God.

"When people take from us with domestic violence and sexual abuse, they leave this void and you have to decide what to fill it with. You can fill it with the lies and the self-loathing and the fear. The fear is debilitating," she said. "My relationship with God was not a choice; it was a necessity."

Theresa describes her process of healing as something that will continue throughout her life.

"Healing hurts. It's going to hurt because you have to relive it one more time so that you can get over it," she said. "Healing brings freedom and you know you're free when you can bring up these horrific things and not lose your mind."

Theresa is now in a healthy marriage, homeschools her children, and stays involved in her church. She uses art as a way to cope with the trauma she experienced. She plans on getting her bachelor's degree.

"My story is victory over the enemy," she said. "People who have hurt me, they don't get to win. My life is to be used for God's will."

Theresa now houses families that are escaping abuse and mentors girls and women experiencing abuse. She does not seek these people out but finds those being abused reaching out to her. She remembers what it was like to feel alone and wants to be the helping person for others that she never had.

"When you get to that point where you look back and it doesn't wreck you anymore, you should be looking back with a flashlight and saying 'Hey, sister, come on through,'" she said.

Theresa hopes that by sharing her story, those abused will feel empowered to find their own freedom and voice.

"Once you get through [domestic abuse], your story is not for nothing. Your story will be encouragement for somebody else, and I hope that is what my story is," Theresa said. "Victimhood steals your voice. One of the most beautiful parts of life is watching people find their voice again."

It Haunts Me

By Amanda Paradis

Heather Vargas realized something was wrong the first time she met Kyle's friends. She remembered, "It takes a lot for me to meet people. I didn't want to go inside." While Vargas contemplated entering the house, Kyle grabbed a can of Mace and sprayed her in the face, the first instance of abuse but far from the last. Vargas endured Kyle's abuse for five years. Vargas had no support system during this period. She lost friends because her entire life centered around him. She was afraid to tell her parents about the abuse, and she became distanced from them.

Kyle not only abused her physically, he abused her verbally, emotionally, and financially. He often called her a "bitch," "slut," or "whore." Hearing these hurtful words repeatedly took a toll on Heather and altered the way she viewed herself. She paid all the bills while Kyle spent money on his "toys," such as his truck and WaveRunners. Kyle's friends and parents were aware of his abusive behavior. In several instances, Kyle's mother witnessed her son pulling Vargas' hair and did nothing to stop the abuse.

Her abuse ended when Kyle committed suicide. Even 18 years later, she still struggles to tell the story because her memory of it is so vivid: Kyle wanted to talk to her, but she felt unsafe – she was afraid of him.

Heather Vargas

"You are a better person, and there is someone out there who will love you for who you are."

She was willing to talk to him outside their house, but she refused to be alone with him. Kyle told Vargas he was going to commit suicide; however, in the past he repeatedly threatened to commit suicide in attempts to make her feel guilty. Because of this pattern, she did not take his threat seriously and went to her parents' house. When she returned to the house she and Kyle shared, she saw it was dark inside – she heard loud music that seemed to be skipping. In that moment she knew. She retreated to a neighbor's house and called the police, who found his body.

She continues to ask herself what she could have done differently that day. On top of this guilt, Kyle's parents also blame Vargas for their son's suicide. The trauma of her abuse continues to affect her everyday life. She suffers from Post Traumatic Stress Disorder and anxiety, has a hard time trusting others, and even jumps at noises. Recently she was living with family members who argued a lot. Their constant yelling and slamming of doors overwhelmed her. She left because the living situation was bringing back bad memories of her time with Kyle.

Vargas is still dealing with and processing the abuse she experienced. Some days are better than others, but she still suffers from anxiety. Counseling has helped her over the years, but this interview was the first time she discussed her abuse with someone outside of a counseling setting. She recognizes healing is a long process. Vargas said Kyle made her feel as if she did not deserve love, but she has finally found a person who loves her. Vargas' advice to others facing similar situations is to walk away and get help. She explained, "You are a better person, and there is someone out there who will love you for who you are."

"Scars Like White Tiger Stripes"

By Tyler James McMaster

Sarah Rivera knew that she and her second husband, Charles, should not have interacted from the moment she saw him. They were both in recovery from addiction and living in a halfway house. Yet, she saw that he shared similar values, was going to church, and working through recovery. Rivera explained that she often values spending time with someone before entering a relationship, but in this instance she threw caution to the wind. They had only been seeing each other for three months. As she puts it, "I saw somebody over the short term, but I didn't see somebody over time."

Once they married and moved in together, Charles immediately relapsed and began to express abusive tendencies. Rivera explained that her first marriage — which lasted for 15 years — was also abusive. She felt as though she could utilize some of her medical training to combat Charles' behaviors, specifically reverse psychology.

Despite her efforts, his abuse continued. In one incident, she wanted to purchase a puppy for Charles, knowing he had desired a pet. However, when she returned with the dog, he was angry that she did so without him. Punching her was his response.

His violence escalated one night when Rivera returned home. She could not remember what sparked the argument, but he suddenly grabbed her by the head and thrust it repeatedly into the edge of the stove. She wanted desperately to go to the hospital so that she could alert the doctors and get the help she needed, but Charles refused. He would not leave her side for the rest of the night. She eventually would get outside and be seen by some neighborhood kids, who then called the police. Charles was arrested but would be released shortly thereafter, charged with simple assault. To protect herself, Rivera acquired a Protection From Abuse Order (PFA).

"He predictably violated the PFA several times," she said, and eventually he went to prison. However, she had not ceased her communication with him. She saw him as someone who needed guidance, stating, "When someone else is in that position, I want to help them." At the time, Charles was expressing in letters that he wanted to get help and sought to change. Once he was released from prison, she allowed him back into her life, but it was quickly evident that he had not changed.

One night Charles had promised that he was going to speak with his sponsor but instead let himself into Rivera's apartment. When she came home, he threw his body into the door, locking her inside. Rivera was on the phone with her mother at the time, so she told her to call the police as soon as possible. Rivera then tried in earnest to calm Charles down, but his rage only grew.

It was becoming clear to her that there was no avoiding an altercation with him, but before she could do much else, Charles grabbed a kitchen knife and stabbed Rivera in the lung. He proceeded to stab her 35 more times in many vital areas all over her body. As much as she pleaded with him, he would not let up. She eventually pretended to be dead so that he would move away from her. Once a window of opportunity opened up, she mustered what was left of her strength and exited the house, screaming for help.

Rivera's graphic detail comes from her current detachment from the situation. "I'm far past it now," she said as a matter of fact. She feels as though she has long since healed and can be as candid with her story as possible. It turned out that she required six to seven units of blood. She suffered an aneurysm, was paralyzed on her left side, and had nine coils in her artery. She would need months of speech therapy afterward and had developed severe Post Traumatic Stress Disorder (PTSD). Rivera also joked that she provided herself with her own care in the ambulance because the EMTs were "inexperienced."

Despite this horrifying episode, Rivera still felt as though she needed to make amends with Charles. "I keep touching fire when it's hot. I've always done

Using Zoom, Staff Writer Tyler McMaster interviews Sarah Rivera (on computer screen).

that," she laughs. As part of her healing, she felt it was important to understand what she may have done to evoke such a violent response from him. She opened up communication once again, trying to get to the deeper issues of his behavior. This would warrant pushback from Charles, leading to further violent outbursts. His words were what finally helped her to understand that there was no way to truly reach him.

She collected all of the letters and correspondence and sent them to the authorities, to put him into prison. Most of this story took place over the course of five months in 2012, but the trial would not take place until 2016. "He just kept coming up with excuses," she explained. She wasn't entirely sure of the exact sentence he received, but she believes it to be 12–29 years.

Currently, Rivera feels better than ever. Her experience has earned her plenty of scars, but she shows them willingly, the white lines her own tiger stripes, so to speak. She does definitely feel desensitized from the situation and recognizes it as a strength and a weakness. She is aware that it affects her interpersonal relationships, as well as her relationship with her children, but also wears it as a badge of pride. She owns what mistakes she may have made in the past and does not regret how she worked toward healing.

Rivera now works with women who are trying to overcome addiction. At the moment of the interview, she was attending a drug and alcohol convention as a director of nursing. "My life is restored," she says, almost peacefully. She acknowledges she still has work to do, but her faith has been a guiding light throughout her life. "I walk in faith, not fear," she beamed. For so much of her life, she was living for herself, but now she makes her decisions based on God and wants to help others through faith.

When asked what she would like to impart to readers and survivors alike, she focused on forgiveness. She feels that survivors should forgive their abusers. "Where were you wrong?" was a question she repeated several times. Accountability is important to her, and she constantly checks her awareness. "Own your shit," was one of her final sentiments. As raw as those words may seem, it exemplifies her "hardcore" spirit. To be able to own one's scars is challenging, but Sarah Rivera has shown us that it's not impossible.

From Victim to Victor

By Maria Trovato

Maria Trovato, Staff Writer (right), interviews Laura Hanrahan.

#FactsMatter

Every 8 minutes, the victim is a child.

Source: RAINN.org

Laura Hanrahan was probably 6 or 7 years old when she first realized that her father was sexually abusing her. She remembered developing ways to shield her body from his advances and the helplessness she felt when she could not stop them.

Hanrahan's father was an alcoholic with an anger problem. Her three siblings suffered his physical abuse, while Hanrahan suffered his sexual abuse. To escape the trauma occurring within her home, she entered a bad relationship and eloped when she

During this time, she had to explain to her children why she was so distraught and acting strangely. Her daughter then confided in her that Hanrahan's father had sexually abused her as well.

Hanrahan was unable to press charges due to the statute of limitations for crimes of a sexual nature. Her daughter would have been able to press charges, but she would have had to testify against her grandfather. Unwilling to do so, her daughter is still searching for a sense of justice.

"There is healing; there is hope in moving from victim to victor," Laura said. "You are not what happened to you."

was 18 years old. During that relationship, Hanrahan regularly abused marijuana and alcohol to try to feel normal.

"He was not the right man for me, but he was a way out," she said. "It was on my wedding night that I saw I made a mistake."

That night, the couple had plans to celebrate with friends, but instead her husband left to snort cocaine. Hanrahan knew it was not a good situation, but at that point she could not go back home.

Hanrahan and her first husband had two kids together. By the time the children were 1 and 3 years old, he started to display anger and violence similar to her father's behavior. Her husband would punch holes in walls and throw the children's toys. Hanrahan's son suffered from colic. She attributes many of her son's ailments to the unhealthy environment.

Hanrahan realized she needed to leave the marriage when her husband forcibly threw her son into his crib. She kicked him out that day, and they eventually got a divorce.

"My kids are not growing up like that," she insisted.

Hanrahan later found real love with her second husband, with whom she has a healthy relationship to this day. With him, she gave birth to another son.

Yet despite the safety she felt with her current husband, when his chest hair turned gray Hanrahan started to have flashbacks of her father. She suffered an emotional breakdown and struggled with suicidal thoughts. Remembering that she wanted her children to have a mother allowed her to survive.

Hanrahan asserted that the statute of limitations and other laws surrounding sexual abuse need to be reevaluated. She explained that as a child, she struggled to understand her abuse. It was only as an adult that she was strong enough to take legal action against her father; by that point, the laws would not allow it.

"We live in a patriarchal society," she said. "The laws protect perpetrators, not victims."

With the birth of her third son, Hanrahan found a strong relationship with God that helped her to heal. Her faith allowed her to forgive her father and reconcile her relationship with her mother.

She was also able to cope with the lack of justice for herself and her daughter.

"Since nothing was done through the humanity of the culture and the legal system here, I still know that justice will have been served at the foot of the cross in heaven," Hanrahan said. "That was freeing."

Learning to talk through her feelings with others also allowed her to heal. When her children were adults, she talked to them about what they all lived through and answered their questions.

"My brain, after growing up like that, learned to put up walls of emotional defense," she said. "Years later, I am starting to develop more honest and intimate relationships with my children."

Hanrahan is also learning to identify and stop her thoughts of self-blame and doubt. She is living the life she always wanted but did not allow herself to dream of. She wants other victims to know that they too can find happiness again.

"There is healing; there is hope in moving from victim to victor," Laura said. "You are not what happened to you."

Kevin MacLean

Refusing to Lie

By Marissa Dunbar

Before Kevin MacLean could remember, he was growing up with an abusive family. His father, an alcoholic, would be sexually abusive towards Kevin's sisters. His mother, a conservative Catholic, neglected the emotional abuse Kevin was receiving. He grew up being the scapegoat for his siblings.

One of Kevin's first experiences involving sexual abuse happened when he was younger. His neighbor invited him over and they later took a trip to the woods. Without Kevin's consent, his neighbor wanted him to perform acts. Immediately, Kevin became ill from fright and ran home.

The abuse began when Kevin's father would playfully tickle one of his sisters until it became inappropriate. As a third grader, this caused confusion for Kevin. After multiple incidences, Kevin would leave the room. "I knew they were all at risk," he says when describing his sisters. At this point, Kevin's mother suspected little to none of her husband's actions.

The abuse at home followed Kevin to school. His teachers would emotionally abuse him which gave his peers the approval to do the same. However, Kevin was relentless and continued to stand up for himself. As a child, he refused to lie. This caused him to get in trouble throughout the years, even though his intentions were moral. Learning martial arts gave him the opportunity to protect himself as no one else would.

Years later, a tragedy would impact Kevin's life forever. As he was walking home one evening, a drunk driver struck and injured Kevin. As a result of the accident, he wore a cast on his leg for approximately 18 months. This meant 18 months of harassment, psychological abuse, and emotional abuse at home. Typically, Kevin only went home to sleep because he wanted to avoid conflict, so this was a difficult time for him. He never fully healed from this injury, producing a permanent limp in his walk.

As a few more years of emotional abuse passed by, one night changed his family's life forever. Kevin was in his room, sharpening a knife he owned with no intentions of harming anyone or anything. His father came in, drunk, and lost his temper when he saw the knife. He immediately swiped the knife out of Kevin's hand. As his father stumbled onto him, Kevin feared for his life. He escaped out of his room and did not come home until the next morning. When Kevin returned, his mother hugged him and apologized for the father's action. He was surprised to learn his father had been kicked out.

Throughout college, Kevin took a wide variety of classes and excelled. Once Kevin finished college, companies wanted to hire him because of his significant knowledge regarding technology. Although he was hired, he would often think of more efficient strategies to better the company. Kevin's co-workers and supervisors would become jealous, causing them to do whatever they could to get him fired. The act of framing was a key factor that led to losing jobs. Once again, Kevin became the scapegoat.

In recent years, Kevin rekindled his relationship with one of his estranged sisters. Upon talking, he recalled the night his father had been kicked out. As he told his story, she also told hers. That same night as the incident with the knife, their mother found his sister's journal. The journal included logs of her molestation episodes she experienced from their father. That is when their mother knew their father had to go. This knowledge later motivated Kevin's mother to advocate helping others find love.

Long-term effects on the mind and body come from any sort of abuse. Kevin suffers from Post Traumatic Stress Disorder, depression, and anxiety. He continues to be hesitant when befriending people because he has become sensitized from them turning on him.

To cope with the stress, Kevin involves himself in art. Getting lost for hours in an activity that produces beauty helps him heal. Kevin does go to therapy, but describes it as "taking an aspirin." Therapy, for him, only helps for a limited amount of time.

"Domestic Violence has driven me to a place where I would like to help everyone in any situation," says Kevin. When given the opportunity, he looks forward to advocating against domestic violence.

Tyler McMaster, Staff Writer, interviews Yessenia Blanco (right).

A Chorus No Longer Silenced

By Tyler James McMaster

Resilience is the word Yessenia Blanco used to describe her story and experiences with domestic violence. She was calm and collected, initially expressing interest in Writing Wrongs and its goals for this year. Her inquiry showed the candor and gentleness of her overall demeanor. No one would expect from her smile the horrors that she has experienced in her life.

Blanco, 34, shared her story as a way to help others who have faced domestic violence. "Everybody has their own perceptions that are so far away from reality," is how she began, immediately staking her position in the conversation. She wants people to know that there is so much more to a survivor's story. The systems and structures that exist and perpetuate violence between partners need to be challenged.

Within her first marriage, she felt as though there was a tension between "who I was and what he believed I was." She wasn't aware of the signs that would lead to eventual violent behavior; she just assumed it was how the relationship should work. While growing up in El Salvador, cultural narratives taught her the purpose of the wife was to serve the "macho man" husband, and while coming to America taught her that these ideas are not wholly acceptable, she feels that some things are just too hard to unlearn.

Events came to a head in their relationship when he one night flung a chair at her head, almost harming her daughter as well. This was when she knew she needed to get away. At the time, she had been working as a case manager for families in similar situations as hers, but she couldn't see the red flags in her own relationship until the violence manifested. Shortly after the incident, she escaped from her husband but wasn't entirely away from the situation.

"It will often take up to 10 times for the victim to leave." A terrifying figure, but very true to many experiences. Blanco discussed the many factors that color this statistic: financial constraints, fear of violence, and safety. These factors often bring victims back to the danger.

She returned to her first husband a few times, but ultimately found solace in her second relationship many years later. He made her feel safe — as though she could fly — wrapped up in a euphoria that can trap survivors in another abusive situation. Within this relationship, the abuse was more subtle, far harder to pick up on than physical violence. "It's about control," she said. The ultimate goal of the abuser is being in control of how their partner lives their life.

At this time, Blanco returned to law school, so she could help others more than the advocacy she previously participated in. Her job as a case manager was earning her a healthy amount of money, while her husband was having some trouble trying to find work. The couple ultimately decided to have her husband stay home and look after their daughters while she worked. It would turn out that this was not the best decision.

She began to notice that basic household chores were not being attended to. Upon arriving home, she would be expected to make dinner because "that's what a wife

how he cornered her for his attack. He threw her against furniture and beat her to the point of death, threatening to kill her if she screamed.

When she awoke, she was surrounded by paramedics. The damage to her body was substantial, but how his violence affected her brain is the true horror. She needed a doctor for every part of her body, including speech therapists, dental professionals, orthopedic surgeons, and even neurologists. Her church mother drove her to appointments and errands because she could barely get around on her own. Confined to walkers and other aids, Blanco was realizing that her life would never be the same. While her husband had not killed her spirit, she would never be the same person again.

Her memory is the biggest worry. While doctors had

"There is always a way out. There are always people who are willing to help; whether it is a church or local shelter, people will always help you."

does." One day she decided to open up over the phone to her "church mother," a woman who was always helpful to Blanco after leaving her first husband. Blanco felt as though she was complaining about her husband's lack of help.

Her husband later confronted her, asking why she shared their issues with her friend. How could he have known they were speaking to one another? As it turned out, he had downloaded software on her phone that monitored her phone calls and text messages; this software was rather complex for 2011.

Naturally this news upset her, prompting Blanco to want to seek counseling. However, her husband felt as though he didn't need any help, and there was nothing wrong with his wanting to keep tabs on his wife. She would not stand for this behavior and resolved to separate if he would not change. This fueled his rage and resentment more.

Shortly after this event, Blanco attended a work party to welcome some levity from their issues. She allowed herself to drink and have some fun but received a rather worrisome text message from her husband when she hadn't answered his calls. A co-worker drove her home. Almost immediately following her return, her husband took her keys and phone, and his fist met her cheek. Then it came again and again and again. "He must have planned it all out," she recalled, not realizing

recommended that she rest her brain to prevent further damage from taking place, she had no choice but to work. She is now a single mother trying to keep her family financially stable. Though she was warned that overstimulation would cause her to lose large portions of her memory, she has had little choice because there aren't many resources for survivors of domestic violence.

Despite these issues, her faith and resilience have kept her fighting for her "new normal." She has utilized her work experiences to seek out activism and social work in the state of Pennsylvania to help other survivors. She cited organizations like the Pennsylvania Coalition Against Domestic Violence, the Lancaster County Domestic Violence Service, and the Office of Victim Advocacy, to name a few. These are all organizations that offer resources of all kinds to help survivors, as well as victims, try and distance themselves from the danger.

When asked what words she may want to share with other survivors and victims, she immediately stated, "There is always a way out. There are always people who are willing to help; whether it is a church or local shelter, people will always help you." Blanco's story joins a chorus of women who are affected by domestic violence, but she will not allow herself to be silenced.

Yessenia Blanco

Amy

An Army of Identities: Coping with DID

By Michaela Yurchak and Marissa Dunbar

"Most people don't have the capacity to fully appreciate what it means to be an atheist and a Christian at the same time. They don't know what it's like to be homophobic and homosexual at the same freakin' time. There is so much I can appreciate," said Amy, a 42-year-old sexual assault survivor with Dissociative Identity Disorder (DID). For privacy purposes, she has chosen not to use her last name.

Amy expressed the rewards as well as the problems of living with DID from childhood trauma. Although she recognized the disorder only four years ago, her trauma began at a very young age. When Amy was about 4 years old, her grandfather and his friends began to sexually assault her in hotel rooms. Not only was she sexually abused, she was also emotionally abused by her father and neglected by her mother. As Amy explained, "She did not bother to protect me."

The assaults left Amy with a lifetime of trauma and an army of alter identities, an army that she currently uses to her advantage as a coping mechanism and a way to learn more about her own experiences.

A total of 21 identities have surfaced throughout her life. While some left and may return, there are about nine that remain. One of them is 5-year-old Charlotte, who is very funny and outgoing. Charlotte tends to come out every day and even made an unforgettable appearance during the interview. Through her light stutter, she shared that she loves sleeping and her favorite color is blue.

Teddy, another of Amy's identities, is a young boy who does not make an appearance too often. Interestingly, Teddy also has an identity named Henry. According to Amy, Henry has only shown up three times. Another identity named Elise is a 12-year-old girl who is very suicidal.

Amy explained that she is conscious while she switches between alters as if she is sitting in the background listening.

Blending, which can be a little more complicated, is when Amy and the alter identity come together as one identity. During this time there can be moments of memory loss and confusion. Amy says, "I can't function. I'm blended with her; it's not me watching. I am her. I am five."

Amy's biggest piece of advice to other survivors dealing with DID is this: "You are not crazy. It is really hard, but it is also this tremendous gift that most people don't have." The disorder can be extremely exhausting, but she expresses how much her alter identities have helped her heal from her trauma.

There are many different triggers that can bring about her alter identities, but the most prominent is speaking about the abuse she endured at the hands of her grandfather.

When asked about coping methods for her triggers, Amy had one word for us: art. Her artwork illustrates her emotional journey through all of this and other events in her and her alters' lives. Therapy also continues to be a key step in the process of coping. Amy has spoken at events such as Break the Silence and venues such as Rest Stop Rejuvenate. Last but certainly not least, her kids are her biggest motivation to continue through this unique life.

"I make [Dissociative Identity Disorder] look easier than it is," says Amy. While the disorder can be incredibly debilitating, most people can have a functioning life while struggling through their identities. Amy is a mother, a wife, a friend, and an advocate. One word Amy used to describe herself as a survivor is inspirational, because she continuously tries to motivate other survivors through her positive outlook about DID.

Amy discusses her art.

26 | Writing Wrongs 2018

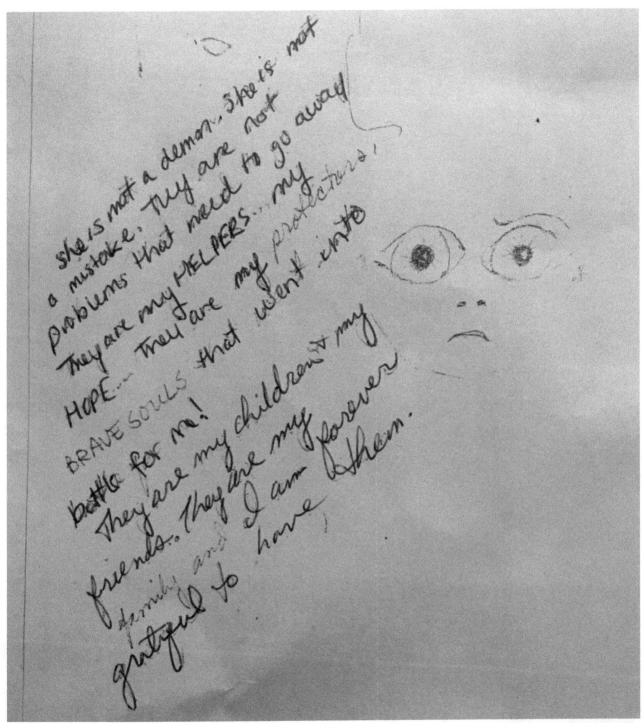

"She is not a demon. She is not a mistake. They are not problems that need to go away. They are my HELPERS…my HOPE. They are my protectors, BRAVE SOULS that went into battle for me! They are my children and my friends. They are my family and I am grateful to have them." — Amy

Rachel Farrow

Growing Beyond the Cracks

By Adam Varoqua

Rachel Farrow, 24, an Outreach Educator for Turning Point of Lehigh Valley, gave the Writing Wrongs staff a description of the organization's services and her own story as a survivor. She is the survivor of two abusive relationships, affected by physical, emotional, sexual, and financial abuse. Turning Point is an organization dedicated to domestic violence survivor advocacy. Their mission reads, "Eliminate Domestic Violence in the Lehigh Valley Through Empowerment, Education, and Engagement."

Farrow elaborated on her role and survivor story. "I am an Outreach Educator so I work here and do prevention education in Lehigh and Northampton counties, and I'm also a survivor of teenage dating violence. So in that regard, I have been on both sides where I am trying to help people recognize the signs as well as someone who has been through it from the time I was 17."

She met her first abuser online in her senior year of high school. From her description, he was at first every girl's dream: he played in a band, had a guitar and a car. This dream turned into a nightmare as Farrow explained, "He cheated on me with 47 different women. He infected me with various diseases. He physically, mentally, emotionally, financially abused and assaulted me." She further told how he prevented her from continuing her education at that time and cut her off from her social group. "When it came time for him to start raping me, sexually harassing me, taking my money, the only people who were allowed in my life to see what was happening were people he chose to put there."

Farrow left him when she was 19 and ended up living in her car for a while because she had nowhere else to go. This was when the start of the second relationship happened, as her second abuser offered to pay rent at an apartment for Farrow to stay in. This relationship was abusive as well, with her abuser's alcoholism supported by taking money from Farrow's paychecks.

As with the first relationship, she found the strength to leave her abuser and begin her path of healing.

Her recovery from all this abuse and trauma came in part from the support and services she received from Turning Point of Lehigh Valley. During the tour, Farrow emphasized the need for survivors to develop beyond their abuse, saying, "You grow or you die." And grow she did. She is now happily married and continuing her education.

Survivors like her walk through Turning Point's doors every day, usually referred by the local police. The referrals begin with domestic calls, as a local officer described. These calls can often be violent, but once officers are dispatched, the victim is often given a "victim's form" that informs them of their rights following the situation. They are then pointed in the direction of Turning Point, which the department works with specifically in the area.

Training to handle domestic calls is completed in the police academy, but officers often do not receive supplementary training on site. Role play and staged scenarios are used to prepare officers for varying situations. "We often handle each call as we see it," the officer stated. He emphasized that every call can be different, so they try to approach all incidents with caution and candor.

To identify the primary aggressor, there is a preliminary investigation that must follow the initial call. However, if there are visible signs of injury, the perpetrator will be arrested on site. "Even if the victim doesn't want to press charges, the arrest is still made."

Once victims report what happened to them, they are referred to Turning Point for their resources and services. As Farrow detailed, all services provided by the agency are free and confidential. Their services include the following: counseling, court advocacy, support groups, an emergency shelter, children's programs, and referrals to other organizations.

To fully advocate for survivors in the area, the organization has a hotline available 24/7 that offers free information and service options.

Farrow showed us additional resources in the waiting room where their staff has brochures and pamphlets available for those waiting to meet with a counselor. Those pamphlets emphasize identification of healthy relationships as well as signs of abuse and the importance of consent.

While Farrow was giving a tour of the facility, our group noticed signs indicating LGBTQ+ community support and bilingual resources in Spanish available for all to see and use, validating the organization's mission to serve all community members who walk through their doors.

One of the most essential services of Turning Point has to be its emergency shelter. At the Turning Point administrative facility, there are supplies for that shelter including school resources for children, feminine hygiene products, food, water, clothes, books, and other basic resources.

At that point in the day, the tour had ended, but the story continues with Farrow's personal growth – the same growth the workers of Turning Point want to impart to all survivors. Through their dedication to victim advocacy, the people of Turning Point help to provide the survivors with the tools needed to be the gardeners of their own lives.

Each of Rachel's tattoos represents a significant incident in her life.

30 | Writing Wrongs 2018

Rachel Farrow

A Relentless Spirit

By Tyler James McMaster

Freshman year of college is typically framed as a formative time in young people's lives. Administrators dole out tired clichés about how collegiate life will forever change students through awkward scholastic soul-searching. This was true for Michaela, whose experience of this kind of self reflection resurfaced past trauma. Despite this difficult beginning to her higher education, Michaela would face her traumas head-on, changing her life for the better and inspiring her to advocate for other survivors of sexual assault and emotional abuse.

He showed his true colors rather quickly, inflicting emotional abuse and exerting control over Michaela for a year. Whenever she felt uncomfortable in a sexual situation, the boyfriend would use her traumas against her, saying that she shouldn't hold onto her past and use it as an "excuse." He would invalidate her pain so he could get what he wanted.

Even when Michaela would attempt to leave the relationship, the boyfriend would threaten suicide. One night, when she tried to leave his car, he locked the doors and threatened even further violence. He

> *"I may get exhausted; I may want to give up; I may not want to be here anymore; but there is this little voice in my subconscious that says, 'You need to do this.'"*

"I never figured out the trigger," she said, recalling the moment her past returned to her. She was suddenly transported back to her mother's house when she was 10 years old. Her parents had recently divorced, and she was primarily living with her mother, who was addicted to drugs at the time. As Michaela recounted, "She had off and on boyfriends in the house constantly," yet one specific boyfriend began to grope and touch Michaela inappropriately. His advances eventually led to assault. Yet, it was not his actions that hurt her the most, but the fact that her mother sat idly by while the event took place.

The sense of betrayal is something that Michaela remembers most vividly, explaining, "Your mom is supposed to be the one who protects you and gets you through." She felt as though the absence of her mother was an absence of a protector in her life.

Michaela had also begun to date someone at school in her freshman year. He was in the local hardcore music scene and almost four years older than she was.

also used sex addiction as an excuse for his frequent cheating and attempted to turn her against her family.

The couple finally separated at the beginning of Michaela's sophomore year. The boyfriend claimed that she abused him and tried to turn other people against her, despite the fact that she had evidence incriminating him.

Once she distanced herself from these events, she moved toward healing. Her college campus offers free therapy resources, which she has utilized since freshman year. She also explored a form of treatment called Eye Movement Desensitization and Reprocessing (EDMR). A patient is asked to recount traumas, and a series of vibrations will be administered "back and forth" to transition thoughts away from the triggers. For Michaela, this treatment helped to ease the pain of her traumas.

Through this therapy, she found that her mom was the biggest trigger to her trauma and that much of her depression stemmed from their relationship.

#FactsMatter

55 percent of sexual assaults occur at or near the victim's home.

— Source: NSVRC.org

These EDMR treatments granted Michaela the peace of acceptance of no relationship with her mother, ultimately easing her depression and anxieties.

When asked to describe her most beneficial support systems, Michaela cited her current boyfriend who remains a constant source of comfort and support throughout her journey and schooling. Another source of empowerment is actually telling her story. "It can be so empowering," she states, expressing that the number one healing factor has been helping others. Working with other survivors and participating in different forms of activism has helped her to regain her voice. Healing becomes easier through these strategies and allows her to see her own physical growth.

To conclude, Michaela described her overall journey in a single word: "Relentless." Despite constant tests to her strength and trust, she pushed onward to find her peace. Her past and present may have changed the person she is, but she remains an empowered activist and staunch ally to women healing from sexual, emotional, and domestic violence. "I may get exhausted; I may want to give up; I may not want to be here anymore; but there is this little voice in my subconscious that says, 'You need to do this.'" She uses this voice every single day to empower others and does not seem to have any intention of stopping.

Staff Writer Michaela Yurchak shares her own story with fellow writer Tyler McMaster.

Kate DeArmas (left) and her sister, Julie Wahl

Healing Through Trauma

By Michaela Yurchak

Kate DeArmas is a 38-year-old mental health therapist who uses her own abuse to bring about positivity and advocacy. After being sexually and physically abused by her ex-husband throughout their 10-year relationship, she finds her healing in nature and helping other survivors.

DeArmas says she finds comfort in "allowing someone to have a space that is safe, even if it is just safe for them for an hour once a week where they can come and talk about it."

Leaving an abuser takes a great deal of strength and courage, especially when victims have been conditioned to believe no one is on their side. Perpetrators often create a barrier between the victim and their families in order to keep their power, and DeArmas' story was no different. "It is important to talk about it but what is hard is [survivors] end up so isolated and the longer it goes on, the more isolated you get. It becomes normal," DeArmas explained.

Because of the isolation imposed by her abuser, she completely lost her relationship with her family, especially her younger sister, Julie, who accompanied her during her interview for support. Julie relayed that her sister would often disappear off the radar and later reestablish contact. But she also conveyed that "Kate finds strength in her own vulnerability," which means she was able to turn those experiences of isolation into a strength.

Healing can be a very long and difficult process for survivors, and DeArmas slowly regained the strength to tell her story and empower others. DeArmas said life can go on for survivors after their assault, especially with proper coping skills. "It's not a death sentence. It doesn't have to be how your life is forever. It doesn't have to continue," she said.

Although helping others can be therapeutic, she also explained the complications that come with her job. "There is such a fine line because being able to

help someone and open their eyes about what they are experiencing can also be incredibly dangerous for them," DeArmas said.

Looking back on the abuse, DeArmas realizes how clear the warning signs were. "On really bad nights, when I wasn't sure if I was going to come out the next morning okay, I would text [my friend] and say, 'If I go missing or if something happens, it was him.'"

DeArmas realizes the red flags that were raised during her relationship with her ex-husband but explained how hard it is to see the problems when you are in the situation. Not being able to take a step back and view what is going on from the outside can be extremely difficult for survivors in the moment.

Although survivors can find different outlets for their healing, the trauma never truly goes away. DeArmas is currently pregnant with her fifth child, a girl, and expressed her fears of being pregnant with a girl in a world where women are oppressed and very often the victims of abuse.

"With the first girl, this is probably the most fear I've had with having a child – not birth, not my ability to raise her, but my ability to protect her," she said. "With what is going on in our society with the #MeToo movement and the abuse every day, it is terrifying."

Many women take a variety of precautions to feel safe and protected while doing basic tasks in their everyday lives. DeArmas spoke of this as well, saying, "One of my friends posted something on Facebook about how she used to run and she got chased once so she stopped." DeArmas said, "I wrote a comment about all the things that I do when I go for a run and when I read back over my comment, I was like, 'Oh my God it is scary, all of the precautions I take.'"

It is through her self awareness and understanding of her own vulnerability that DeArmas became strong enough to advocate for others.

Survivor of Steel

By Adam Varoqua

Marjorie Faler, 45, became pregnant at 16. Her boyfriend at that time was 10 years older than she was, and he was already divorced with three children. Before the abuse started, he seemed like an average, calm man. Once he found out that she was pregnant, that's when the problems started. She relayed, "Probably the first time something happened, we were walking the down the street and I looked over as some guys were walking by. He accused me of staring at them."

He started to argue with her and became physical. As she described, "I went to walk away and he just grabbed my arm. It was something simple. That type of thing would continue. Someone would walk by, he

by those around her, not to pursue charges because oftentimes the victims would be murdered by the hands of their abuser before the trial could even begin.

While the physical abuse was awful and threatened the life of her unborn child, it did not end there. She said, "He told me I was never going to leave him. At least not alive."

He threatened her constantly to prevent her from leaving. He would also exert his control over her. For instance, in order not to let her out of his sight, he walked with Faler to meet her mother downtown.

When Faler finally gave birth to her daughter, that's when things started to change for the better. As she

"No matter what it is, you are strong. Indestructible."

would make a comment that I was looking at them, and I wasn't or they were looking at me."

From then on, the physical abuse became worse. "He would start these fights and he would hit me. Punch me in the stomach. Choke me."

The physical and emotional toll of all this was not just affecting Faler but her unborn daughter, too. She said, "Each time it just got progressively worse, to the point where I almost lost my daughter. I had gone to the hospital a couple of times and had to be hooked up to different monitors and things like that to monitor how she was doing because she was threatening to come early." She would continue to go to the hospital multiple times during the course of her pregnancy in fear of a premature birth.

During her anguish at the hands of her abuser, she thought she had no one to turn to and that it was her fault that he was abusive towards her. She also said that when she was a child, she knew a family member suffering from abuse, and the family member was told

said, "I had told him previously that if he didn't get a vasectomy because he had those three previous children and then I had my daughter that I was definitely going to leave. So he had one scheduled that Monday. I made sure he had that done. And then after he had his surgery, and [I] had my daughter, I told him I was leaving him." She also told him that he would have to pay child support. They planned to meet again a couple of days afterward for her to receive a child support payment in order to help her raise her daughter. She planned to expect the worst from him, and her suspicions were confirmed. She recalled, "Because of our history I had taken like a knife, dagger, and put it in my boot and met him. He tried to hug me, he tried to kiss me, tried to get close to me, and I backed away from him and he kicked me in the stomach."

It was at that moment of pain and anger that she kicked him and drew out the knife that she had concealed to try to defend herself.

Marjorie Faler

Staff Writer Adam Varoqua (right) interviews Marjorie Faler.

Since this happened in broad daylight, a bystander called the police. The police weren't as sympathetic as one would think. She explained, "The police blamed me. I had the knife."

She was allowed to go home, where she finally told her mother all that had happened to her. Her mother proceeded to call the police to have Faler explain the abuse that she was suffering from.

An officer came over to the house. Faler stated, "He told me the process on how to file a Protection From Abuse, and then he told me he would stand beside me through this process."

The next day, she visited the attorney in charge of domestic violence cases, who stood with Faler throughout the courtroom process. The judge overseeing the Protection From Abuse Order criticized Faler's actions that day. Faler recalled, "He didn't like the part about me kicking him back or the knife. He said, 'You are not allowed, no matter what happens to you, you are not allowed to do anything back, you are just as bad as the abuser.'"

Regardless, he granted the request, essentially barring the boyfriend from ever seeing Faler, except for child visitations. The first visitation was no ordinary one though, as her abuser strangled Faler in front of her child and his three children. He was taken to jail but continued to harass her through mail and phone calls. After he was released from jail, he always left Faler alone.

The abuse unfortunately did not end there as she entered another relationship with a person with a drinking problem. The second abusive relationship, though, did not last as long as the first. Faler explained, "We had gone camping and we were in the mountains and we did not bring any alcohol with us."

He disappeared on this trip, looking for a drink, which frustrated Faler and caused her to pack up the car and plan to drive off. The perpetrator came back and was upset to see the car packed. Faler remembered, "I woke up to him straddling me and strangling me.

I got away by breaking his nose and stealing the car because it was his car."

While no charges were filed on her for stealing the car, the abuser was not charged at all for what he did that night. As in the first relationship, Faler was able to leave and be free from the perpetrator's abuse.

Faler's journey has not been easy, but there's a lesson that she wants readers to take away. She said, "My biggest thing I want people to know from this is that you are not alone. There's a way out. Even though you feel scared and you feel like you can't tell anyone."

She also emphasized the need for those abused to seek a way out. She shared, "One way or another, there is hope."

Hope is what helped Faler to raise her daughter all by herself. Her daughter is now 28 and is happily married. Hope is what also gave Faler the strength to leave her abusers and gravitate away from her trauma. Transitioning away from her past abuses, Faler has a new perspective on life, saying, "I feel good. I feel good that I survived this because it took a lot to do what I did. It wasn't easy. It's not easy to raise a kid on your own. It's not easy to get away from someone who has been hurting you and tells you that they're going to hunt you down and kill you."

She opened up about her faith in God and how it developed over the years, saying, "I didn't have a strong faith in God but now I do, and I believe He brings you through things for a reason. He puts people in places for a reason."

Her story of survival made her realize that there is a defining trait to all survivors: strength. She expanded on this, saying, "I think a survivor is strong; when you think survivor – strong. Even though they don't feel it, because you don't feel it when you are going through that mess. You feel usually, the term is weak, and you think 'weak' when you are going through it but to survive it? No matter what it is, you are strong. Indestructible."

———————— **#FactsMatter** ————————

Out of every 1,000 sexual assaults, 310 are reported to police.

———————— Source: RAINN.org ————————

My Spirit
By Adam Varoqua

You can spit on me and try to break me
But know my spirit is still free
Berate who I am and what I do
But I remain resolute and true
You may not agree,
But still my spirit is free

I've been knocked down only to rise again,
Understand that for now and then,
My religion is Fire, my actions Inspire,
From this match I have no plans to retire
Something else you may see,
But my spirit is free

My scars and cuts do testify,
I have survived through marching on, this I verify
Look me down all you want to taunt,
At rising above it all, I am a Savant
Hard to believe, yes indeed,
But yet my spirit is free

With your hate I thrive.
Through what I Love, I still strive
I will not slow, I must always go,
I hope you know that this is my own show!
With this I proudly decree!
I am still free!

Advocates Seeking Justice

By Amanda Paradis

The Berks County District Attorney's office has a specialized unit devoted to Domestic Violence and Child Abuse comprised of two attorneys, Meg McCallum and James Goldsmith, and an Outreach/Education Coordinator, Heather Barger. McCallum works with children who have been physically or sexually abused, while Goldsmith works with adults who have been physically or sexually abused. The Berks County District Attorney's office is fortunate enough also to have a Victim/Witness unit, which provides services to those who have been abused and witnesses who may testify. McCallum explained that their line of work is not easy. They have a different dynamic when it comes to how they go about investigating and prosecuting. They have to approach each case with a great degree of sensitivity and wariness due to the potential volatility of the situation. McCallum alluded to the fact that these cases are among the most difficult to process for a variety of reasons: "It is very difficult being a victim of any kind, but when your partner or person who is supposed to be there to help you and protect you is your abuser, it makes it approximately a thousand times worse."

Another aspect that makes processing these cases particularly difficult is that many victims of domestic physical or sexual assault are not always willing to cooperate. Abuse is a cycle; some survivors may be afraid to sit in a courtroom and identify a person as the perpetrator of a cycle of violence. Some may reconcile with their abuser due to financial, emotional, or familial reasons, such as wanting to keep a family together. However, what many individuals are not aware of is that the District Attorney's office represents the Commonwealth; they do not represent the victim. While they are victim advocates, and in many cases, fighting for the victim, ultimately the victim is not the prosecutor's client. In the legal sphere, crimes are considered an offense against society. Since it is viewed as a violation of the state, even if the victim

chooses not to proceed, prosecutors can continue with the case. This can be difficult for some survivors to accept. Prosecutors want to be sensitive to victim's wishes, but at the end of the day, they have an ethical obligation to hold perpetrators of crime responsible regardless of whether the victim desires to go through with it or drop the charges. Ultimately, it is the District Attorney's office that determines whether to pursue or drop the charges. A large determinant of whether or not prosecutors go through with the case is if they believe they can obtain a conviction, thus bringing justice to the victim. Prosecutors have the burden of proof; they need to ensure the judge or jury believes the defendant is guilty beyond a reasonable doubt. Goldsmith stressed one of the most difficult aspects of his job is sitting with a sexual assault survivor and asserting, "I cannot look you in the eye, given all the evidence, [and say] that we would be successful in getting a conviction." Goldsmith explains that, if he cannot do that, he is not doing his job for the victim or for anyone. Why put them through the arduous process of the criminal justice system knowing it may not be a good result for them in the end? Prosecutors want to bring closure to abuse victims. Sometimes the best way to bring closure is to say, "We will not go forward" to avoid dragging it out.

Prosecutors do have legal mechanisms to protect abuse victims who may be in danger. Berks County specifically sets high bails to make it more difficult for perpetrators to be released. In cases where they are released, bail conditions are set. Bail conditions may include guidelines perpetrators must follow, including staying away from the victim. This can be physically staying away or even ensuring they have no verbal contact with the victim. In addition, victims of domestic violence can obtain Protection From Abuse Orders (PFAs). PFAs effectively criminalize any communication or contact between the perpetrator and survivor. If perpetrators attempt to intimidate witnesses into not testifying, then they can be criminally charged. If the victim is in immediate danger, Berks County does have limited funds to relocate victims. This is only used in the most serious cases.

The Victim/Witness unit at the Berks County District Attorney's office was established to assist victims and witnesses through the criminal justice process. Their mission statement includes: "To serve as advocates for the enforcement of fundamental rights of crime victims and promote the belief that all victims and witnesses deserve to be treated with dignity, compassion, and respect throughout the judicial process. ..." Those in the Victim/Witness unit are advocates for survivors. Heather Barger explained that advocates want to do everything in their power to assure that victims and witnesses feel safe and understand the criminal justice process. Victim/Witness Coordinators will attend the preliminary hearing to introduce themselves to the person they will be working with. Given that the victim accepts help, the Victim/Witness Coordinator will explain the judicial system, accompany victims to court if needed, prepare the survivor for court testimony, and even help with writing impact statements. Victim/witness coordinators can also inform and notify victims of case information.

The Berks County District Attorney's office puts forth a great deal of effort. There is no doubt these individuals deal with emotionally jarring cases on a daily basis. Their staff is not only extremely sensitive to their clients' needs, they also provide a unique amount of support to one another. Goldsmith, Barger, and McCallum agree that their colleague support and team effort help them cope with the stress of their profession. Goldsmith stated they are surrounded by people who are all doing what they believe in. Their careers allow them to see the worst in humanity, but also the best in humanity.

Staff Writer Amanda Paradis

Meg McCallum, Assistant DA

Heather Barger, Outreach/Education Coordinator

James Goldsmith, Assistant DA

Meet the Writing Wrongs 2018 Staff

James Burton
Widener University
Print Designer

Marissa Dunbar
Northampton Community College
Writer

Matthew Ludak
Drew University
Photographer

Tyler James McMaster
Kutztown University
Writer

Carlee Nilphai
Millersville University
Alumni Contributor
Social Media Manager

Alexyss Panfile
Montclair State University
Writer

Amanda Paradis
Arcadia University
Writer

Nina Renna
Northampton Community College
Print Designer

Maria Travato
University of Maryland
Writer

Adam Varoqua
Seton Hall University
Writer

Michaela Yurchak
Kutztown University
Writer

Meet the Writing Wrongs 2018 Advisors

Dawn Heinbach
Founder & Program Manager of Writing Wrongs
Freelance Writer and Editor, New Dawn Enterprises, LLC

Dawn graduated summa cum laude from Kutztown University in 2016 with a Bachelor of Arts in English/Professional Writing and minor concentrations in Digital Communication & New Media and Public Relations. She is now a double degree candidate at Rosemont College pursuing an M.F.A. in Creative Writing and an M.A. in Publishing.

Jane Ammon
Lehigh Carbon Community College
Photography

Colleen Clemens
Kutztown University
Writing/Editing

Gayle Hendricks
Northampton Community College
Print Design

Jessica Hughes
Millersville University
Social Media

Michelle Kaschak
Penn State Lehigh Valley
Writing/Editing

Anne Mahar
Arcadia University
Writing/Editing

Janae Sholtz
Alvernia University
Writing/Editing

Donna Singleton
Reading Area Community College
Writing/Editing

Serving people who impact humanity

Humanitarian Social Innovations (HSI) is a nonprofit organization with a humanitarian mission to create social impact through fiscal sponsorship, incubation, and mentorship of early-stage nonprofits and grassroots movements.

HSI's mission is inspiring and connecting social entrepreneurs with the resources necessary to empower them and to maximize their humanitarian impact.

As a part of our *Acceleration – Do Something!* program, Writing Wrongs has full non-profit status. For more information about the relationship between Writing Wrongs and HSI, please visit our website.

hsifiscalsponsor.org

301 Broadway
Box 13 — Suite M100-F
Bethlehem, PA 18015
office@humanitariansocialinnovations.com

 @HumanitarianSocialInnovations

 @hsi_innovators

 @hsi_innovators

What makes us the leading manufacturer of AUTOMOTIVE BATTERIES & ACCESSORIES?

EXPERIENCE

Our employees represent new hires with fresh perspectives working alongside dedicated, long-term team members with expertise in all facets of the business. Over 30 percent of employees have more than 10 years of service, with close to 1,000 of those employees having over 20 years tenure.

INNOVATION

Innovation lets us turn big ideas into better products and solutions that drive value, efficiency and sustainability. It's reflected in our people, our technologies, and our commitment to the environment.

SUSTAINABILITY

Sustainability means designing and manufacturing defect-free, durable products that provide years of performance. We have one of the lowest defect rates in our industry through a deep quality-centered culture and relentless continuous improvement initiatives.

www.eastpennmanufacturing.com

Deka Road

Lyon Station, PA 19536

610-682-6351

Thank you to the Sponsors of the Writing Wrongs 2018 program

Service Sponsor
Hampton Inn

Justice Sponsor
East Penn Manufacturing

Integrity Sponsor
Neumann University

Honesty Sponsors
Healing Works
Dr. Joanne Gabel
Dr. Donna Singleton
Cindy Tricoski

Friend Sponsors

Al Walentis
Balanced Life Counseling
BCTV
Berks County Victim/Witness Assistance Unit
Carlee Nilphai
Charles Holdefer
Cultura Law
Emily Leayman
Giant
Inner Vision Counseling
John Miravitch
Kristin Pedemonti

Laurel House
Mi Casa Su Casa
National Center on Domestic and Sexual Violence
NAMI Berks
Patti Steely
Paula Beltrán Franco
Robin Costenbader-Jacobson
Sweet Ride Ice Cream
Thriveworks
Turning Point of Lehigh Valley
Weis
All who supported our fundraisers

Proudly Supports Writing Wrongs

We thank the contributors who dedicated their time and talents to raise awareness of domestic violence and sexual assault.

P.O. Box 764, Norristown, PA 19404
www.laurel-house.org 24-hour hotline: 800-642-3150

Kutztown

Latino/American Restaurant

Cafe, Comfort, Conversation, Creative Arts

Johanny Cepeda, Owner/Manager
320 Penn St.
Reading, PA 19602

610-375-1161

johannycepeda@gmail.com
Monday – Saturday, 7 a.m. – 4 p.m.

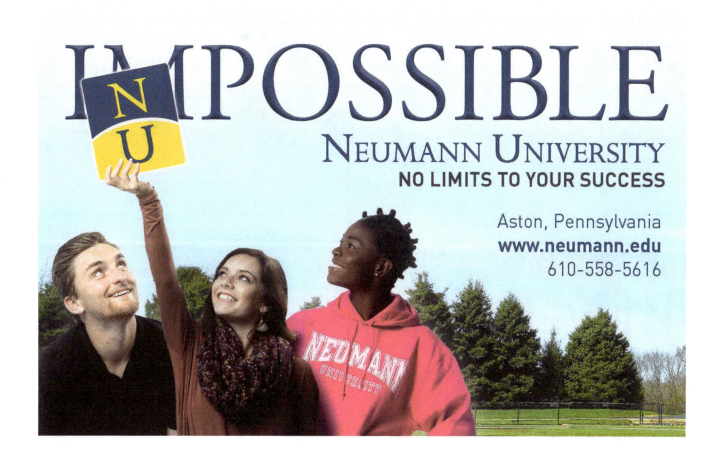

Healing Works

Psychotherapy, healing, recovery for children, teens and families

Celebrating 10 years of Break The Silence
April 2019

1644 W. Walnut Street, rear
Allentown, PA 18102
HealingWorksAllentown.com
healingworks2@outlook.com
610-432-2168

Anne Crothers, M.Ed.
Therapist/Owner

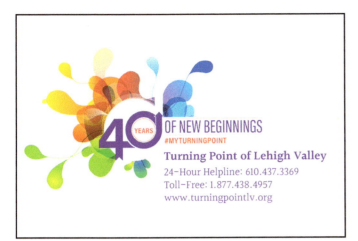

Turning Point of Lehigh Valley
24-Hour Helpline: 610.437.3369
Toll-Free: 1.877.438.4957
www.turningpointlv.org

Abraham J. Cepeda, Esq.
Attorney/Abogado

Bi-Lingual in
Spanish & English

TEL: 610-375-4380
FAX: 484-866-8668

CulturaLaw@gmail.com

Kutztown

Wyomissing

Lisa Speck-Casadei della Chiesa, MA, LPC
Licensed Professional Counselor

255 Butler Avenue, Suite 103
Lancaster, PA 17601

• • •

info@balancedlifelancaster.com

717-875-4528

www. balancedlifelancaster.com

Strength in Vulnerability: Reclaimed Voices of Domestic Violence & Sexual Assault | 51

Fifteen
By Tyler James McMaster

If I could simply impart to you the person you've become,
you would hold belief in the palms of your hands, cradling dreams
turned to nightmares. I still hear the cries and silent sobs, performed
for a singular injury, or suspicious jury; crisp
visions seared within the iris. But I promise you, this ends.

Long years spent stripping bark from the base of your favorite tree.
Building vessels out of vitriol to set sail on caustic seas.
Stray filaments glowing as your switch is left cast downward,
lungs terrified of how they will lie to sense, a weary glance.
Yet, once you learn of your true identity, freedom rides swift

on a cool breeze of reverie. Pink roses flutter open,
breathing in the saccharine of feminine, mirrors cracking
from the weight of prideful, ephemeral fists. Light shining bright
behind your hands and, bringing them to your chest, a faint refrain:
"I was fifteen and calling."

CPSIA information can be obtained
at www.ICGtesting.com
Printed in the USA
BVHW011521130119
537719BV00008B/410/P